DEC 11 2014

Bruno Mars

Cover photo © Tony Nelson / Retna Ltd.

ISBN 978-1-4803-7227-6

HAL•LEONARD®
CORPORATION
7777 W. BLUEMOUND RD. P.O. BOX 13819 MILWAUKEE, WI 53213

In Australia Contact:
Hal Leonard Australia Pty. Ltd.
4 Lentara Court
Cheltenham, Victoria, 3192 Australia
Email: ausadmin@halleonard.com.au

Visit Hal Leonard Online at
www.halleonard.com

Guitar Chord Songbook

Contents

Count on Me

Words and Music by Bruno Mars,
Ari Levine and Philip Lawrence

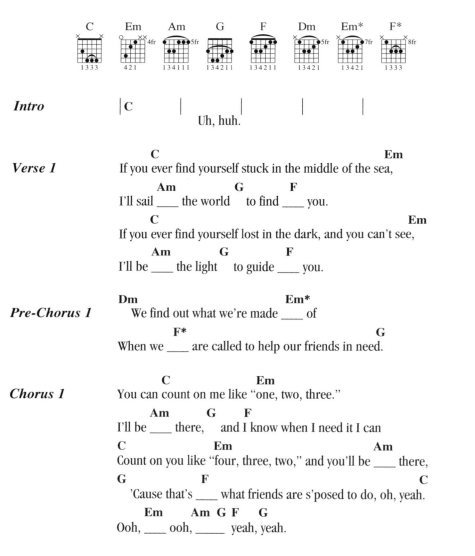

Intro | C | | | |

Uh, huh.

Verse 1

                 C   Em

If you ever find yourself stuck in the middle of the sea,

      Am   G   F

I'll sail ____ the world   to find ____ you.

                 C   Em

If you ever find yourself lost in the dark, and you can't see,

      Am   G   F

I'll be ____ the light   to guide ____ you.

Pre-Chorus 1

Dm   **Em***

We find out what we're made ____ of

        F*   **G**

When we ____ are called to help our friends in need.

Chorus 1

                 C   Em

You can count on me like "one, two, three."

      Am   G   F

I'll be ____ there,   and I know when I need it I can

C   Em   Am

Count on you like "four, three, two," and you'll be ____ there,

G   F   C

   'Cause that's ____ what friends are s'posed to do, oh, yeah.

      Em   Am G F   G

Ooh, ____ ooh, _____ yeah, yeah.

Verse 2

C   Em
If you're tossin' and you're turnin', and you just can't fall asleep,

     Am   G   F
I'll sing ___ a song   beside ___ you.

                 C   Em
And if you ever forget how much you really mean to me,

     Am   G   F
Ev'ry day ___ I will   remind ___ you.

Pre-Chorus 2   *Repeat Pre-Chorus 1*

Chorus 2   *Repeat Chorus 1*

Bridge

      Dm   Em*   Am G
You'll always have my shoulder when you cry.

   Dm   Em*   F
I'll never let go, never say good - bye.

Chorus 3

G   C   Em
You know you can count on me like "one, two, three."

     Am   G   F
I'll be ___ there,   and I know when I need it I can

C   Em   Am
Count on you like "four, three, two," and you'll be ___ there,

G   F   C
  'Cause that's ___ what friends are s'posed to do, oh, yeah.

     Em   Am
Ooh, ___ ooh,

G   F   C
  You can count ___ on me 'cause I can count on you.

Gorilla

Words and Music by Bruno Mars,
Ari Levine and Philip Lawrence

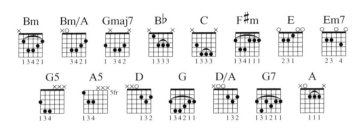

Intro | N.C. |

Verse 1

N.C. **Bm**   **Bm/A**
Ooh, ____ I got a body full of liquor with a cocaine kicker,

                                  Gmaj7
And I'm feelin' like I'm thirty feet tall,

  B♭   **C**
So lay it down, lay it down.

Bm   **Bm/A**
You got your legs up in the sky with the devil in your eyes.

                            Gmaj7
Let me hear you say you want it all.

B♭   **C**
Say it now, say it now.

Pre-Chorus 1

      F#m   Bm   E
Look what you're doin', ____ look what you've done.

                Em7
But in this jungle you can't run,

                G5
'Cause what I got for you, I promise it's a killer.

                A5
You'll be bangin' on my chest, bang, bang, gorilla.

Chorus 1

D   C   G
 (Ooh, ____ hoo, yeah.)

                         Bb   C
You and me, baby, makin' love like go - rillas.

D   C   G
 (Ooh, ____ hoo, yeah.)

                         Bb   C
You and me, baby, makin' love like go - rillas.

Verse 2

Bm   Bm/A
Yeah, got a fistful of your hair, but you don't look like you're scared.

                                       Gmaj7
You just smile and tell me, "Daddy, it's yours,"

      Bb   C
'Cause you know how I like it, you's a dirty little lover.

Bm
If the neighbors call the cops, call the sheriff,

      Bm/A
Call the S.W.A.T., we don't stop.

                                       Gmaj7
We keep rockin' while they're knockin' on our door.

                       Bb   C
And you're screamin', "Give it to me baby, give it to me motherfucker."

Pre-Chorus 2

F#m   Bm   E
Oh, look what you're do - in', look what you've done.

Em7
But in this jungle you can't run,

G5
'Cause what I got for you, I promise it's a killer.

A5
You'll be bangin' on my chest, bang, bang, gorilla.

Chorus 2   *Repeat Chorus 1*

Bridge

F#m   Bm   D/A
I bet you never ever felt so good, so good.

F#m   Bm   D/A
I got your body tremblin' like it should, it should.

G7
You'll never be the same, baby,

A
Once I'm done with you, ooh, ooh, ooh, ooh.

Outro-Chorus

D   C   G
Yeah, ooh, yeah, ooh, hoo, yeah, ooh, hoo.

Bb   C
Oh, you and me, baby, makin' love like go - rillas.

D   C   G
(Ooh, ___ hoo, yeah.)

Bb   C
You and me, baby, we'll be fuckin' like go - rillas.

D   C   G
(Ooh, ___ hoo, yeah.)

Bb   C   D C G Bb C N.C.(D)
You and me, baby, makin' love like go - rillas.

It Will Rain

from the Summit Entertainment film
THE TWILIGHT SAGA:
BREAKING DAWN - PART 1

Words and Music by Bruno Mars,
Philip Lawrence and Ari Levine

Melody:

If you ev - er leave _ me, ba - by,

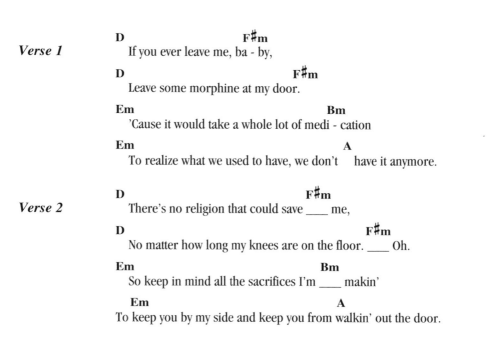

D   F#m   Em   Bm   A   G   Bm/A   F#7

Verse 1

D   F#m
   If you ever leave me, ba - by,

D   F#m
   Leave some morphine at my door.

Em   Bm
    'Cause it would take a whole lot of medi - cation

Em   A
    To realize what we used to have, we don't   have it anymore.

Verse 2

D   F#m
   There's no religion that could save ____ me,

D   F#m
   No matter how long my knees are on the floor. ____ Oh.

Em   Bm
   So keep in mind all the sacrifices I'm ____ makin'

  Em   A
To keep you by my side and keep you from walkin' out the door.

Chorus 1

```
           G                A
'Cause there'll be no sun - light

F#m         Bm  Bm/A
If I lose you, ba - by.

G                    A
There'll be no clear ___ skies

F#m         Bm  Bm/A
If I lose you, ba - by.

G                A          F#7              Bm
Just like the clouds, ___ my eyes ___ will do the same.

      Bm/A       Em                  A          N.C.
If you ___ walk a - way, ev'ry day it'll rain, ___ rain, rain.

D   F#m D  F#m
Ooh. ___ Ooh.
```

Verse 3

```
D                           F#m
  I'll never be your mother's fa - v'rite.

D                              F#m
  Your daddy can't even look me in the eye. ___ Ooh.

Em                         Bm
  If I was in their shoes, I'd be doin' the ___ same thing,

     Em                                A
Sayin' there goes my little girl walkin' with that ___ troublesome guy.
```

Verse 4

           D   **F♯m**
But they're ___ just afraid of something they can't un - derstand. Ooh.

D   **F♯m**
  But, little darlin', watch me change their minds.

                    Em   **Bm**
Yeah, for you I'll try, ___ I'll try, I'll try, I'll try

                    Em
And pick up these bro - ken pieces

                 A
Till I'm bleedin' if that'll make you mine.

Chorus 2   *Repeat Chorus 1*

Bridge

F♯m   **Em**   **F♯m**
  Oh, don't just say ___ (Don't just say.) goodbye. ___ (Goodbye.)

               Em   **F♯m**
Don't just say ___ (Don't just say.) goodbye. ___ (Goodbye.)

               G
I'll pick up these bro - ken pieces

               A
Till I'm bleedin' if that'll make it right.

Outro-Chorus   *Repeat Chorus 1*

Grenade

Words and Music by Bruno Mars,
Ari Levine, Philip Lawrence, Brody Brown,
Claude Kelly and Andrew Wyatt

Melody:

Eas - y come, eas - y go;   that's just how you live.

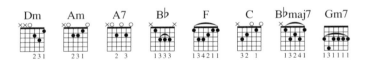

Intro |N.C. |

Verse 1

Dm
Easy come, easy go; that's just how you live.

  Am
Oh, take, take, take it all, but you never give.

Dm
Should've known you was trouble from the first kiss.

  Am   **A7 N.C.**
Had your eyes wide open. Why were they open?

Pre-Chorus 1

Dm
Gave you all I had and you tossed it in the trash.

   Am
You tossed ____ it in the trash, you did.

   Dm
To give ____ me all your love is all I ever asked,

   B♭   **A7**
'Cause ____ what you don't understand ____ is,

Chorus 1

N.C.   **Dm** **B♭**
 I'd catch a grenade ____ for ya,

F **C**   **Dm** **B♭**
 Throw my hand on a blade ____ for ya.

F   **C**   **Dm** **B♭**
 I'd jump in front of a train ____ for ya.

F   **C**   **Dm** **B♭**
 You know I'd do anything ____ for ya.

F **C**   **B♭maj7**   **C**
 Oh, ____ oh, I would go through all this pain,

   F   **A7**   **Dm**
Take a bullet straight through my brain.

C   **B♭**
Yes, I would die ____ for you, baby,

A7 N.C.   **Dm**
 But you won't do the same.

   Am
No, ____ no, no, no.

Verse 2

Dm
Black, black, black and blue, beat me 'till I'm numb.

   Am
Tell the devil I said, "Hey," when you get back to where you're from.

Dm
Mad woman, bad woman, that's just what you are.

    Am   **A7** **N.C.**
Yeah, you'll smile in my face, then rip the brakes out my car.

Pre-Chorus 2 *Repeat Pre-Chorus 1*

Chorus 2

      N.C.   **Dm**   **B♭**
        I'd catch a grenade ____ for ya,

      F   **C**   **Dm**   **B♭**
        Throw my hand on a blade ____ for ya.

      F   **C**   **Dm**   **B♭**
        I'd jump in front of a train ____ for ya.

      F   **C**   **Dm**   **B♭**
        You know I'd do anything ____ for ya.

      F   **C**   **B♭maj7**   **C**
        Oh, ____ oh, I would go through all this pain,

           F   **A7**   **Dm**
    Take a bullet straight through my brain.

    C   **B♭**
    Yes, I would die ____ for you, baby,

    A7 **N.C.**
        But you won't do the same.

Bridge

    Gm7
        If my body was on fire,

    Dm
        Ooh, you'd watch me burn down in flames.

    Gm7
        You said you loved me, you're a liar,

           A7   **Dm** **B♭**
    'Cause you never, ever, ever did, baby.

Chorus 3

A7	N.C.		Dm	Bb

But darlin' I'd still catch a grenade ____ for ya,

F	C		Dm	Bb

Throw my hand on a blade ____ for ya.

F	C		Dm	Bb

I'd jump in front of a train ____ for ya.

F	C		Dm	Bb

You know I'd do anything ____ for ya.

F	C	Bbmaj7		C

Oh, ____ oh, I would go through all this pain,

F	A7	Dm

Take a bullet straight through my brain.

C	Bb

Yes, I would die ____ for you, baby,

A7	N.C.	Dm

But you won't do the same.

Am

No, you won't do the same.

Dm

You wouldn't do the same.

Am

Ooh, you never do the same,

N.C.

No, no, no, no.

If I Knew

Words and Music by Bruno Mars,
Ari Levine and Philip Lawrence

Melody:

Oh, oh, — oh, I, _____

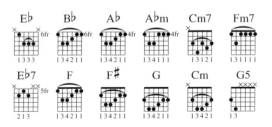

Verse 1

    N.C.   Eb   Bb
Oh, oh, oh, I, I was a city boy,

       Ab
Ride into dangers where I'd always run,

   Abm
A boy who had his fun.

Chorus 1

                Eb Cm7   Fm7
I wouldn't have done all the things that I have done

   Bb   Eb
If I knew one day you'd come.

Ab   Abm   Eb
No, baby, (No, baby,) no, baby, (no, baby.)

Verse 2

B♭ N.C.   E♭   B♭
Oh, oh, oh, I, I know it breaks your heart

         A♭
To picture the only one you want and love

   A♭m
In someone else's arms.

Chorus 2   *Repeat Chorus 1*

Bridge

E♭7 F   F♯ G
    Oh, ba - by, please,

                    Cm
Let's leave the past be - hind us, behind us,

F F♯ G   Cm
So that we can go where love will find us,

Yeah, will find us.

G F♯   F
I   know monsters will leave me,

   G5 A♭   B♭ N.C.
But I   know that you'll be - lieve   me.

Verse 3

    E♭   B♭
Baby, I, I wish we were seventeen

        A♭   A♭m
So I could give you all the innocence   that you give to me.

             E♭   Cm7   Fm7
Oh, I wouldn't have done all ____ the things that I've done

 B♭   E♭
If I knew one day you'd come.

A♭   A♭m   E♭
  If I knew ____ one day you'd come.

Just the Way You Are

Words and Music by Bruno Mars,
Ari Levine, Philip Lawrence,
Khari Cain and Khalil Walton

Melody:

Ah, _____ ah, ah, _ ah, _____

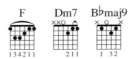

F   **Dm7**   **B♭maj9**

Intro

      F   **Dm7**   **B♭ maj9**   **F**
(Ah, ah, ah, ah, ah, ah, ah, ah, ah, ah, ah.)

Verse 1

        F
Oh, ____ her eyes, her eyes make the stars look like they're not shinin'.

Dm7
Her hair, her hair falls perfectly without her tryin'.

B♭maj9   **F**
She's so beautiful and I tell her ev'ry ____ day. Yeah.

Verse 2

     F
I know, I know when I compliment her she won't believe me.

Dm7
And it's so, it's so sad to think she don't see what I see.

B♭maj9   **F**
But ev'ry time she asks me, "Do I look okay?" I say,

Chorus 1

         F   **Dm7**
When I see your face ____ there's not a thing ____ that I would change.

      B♭maj9   **F**
'Cause you're amaz - ing just the way you are.

            Dm7
And when you smile the whole world stops ____ and stares for a while

      B♭maj9   **F**
'Cause girl, you're amaz - ing just the way you are. ____ Yeah.

Verse 3

  F
  Her lips, her lips, I could kiss them all day if she'd let me.

Dm7
  Her laugh, her laugh she hates but I think it's so sexy.

B♭maj9   **F**
  She's so beautiful and I tell her ev'ry ____ day.

Verse 4

    F
Oh, you know, you know, you know I'd never ask you to change.

  Dm7
  If perfect's what you're searchin' for then just stay the same.

  B♭maj9   **F**
So ____ don't even bother askin' if you look okay, you know I'll say,

Chorus 2

         F   **Dm7**
When I see your face ____ there's not a thing ____ that I would change.

      B♭maj9   **F**
'Cause you're amaz - ing just the way you are.

            Dm7
And when you smile the whole world stops ____ and stares for a while

      B♭maj9   **F**
'Cause girl, you're amaz - ing just the way you are.

        Dm7
The way you are, the way you are.

      B♭maj9   **F**
Girl, you're amaz - ing just the way you are.

Outro-Chorus *Repeat Chorus 1*

The Lazy Song

Words and Music by Bruno Mars,
Ari Levine, Philip Lawrence and
Keinan Warsame

Melody:

To - day I don't feel like do - in' an - y-thing.

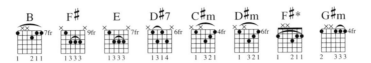

Chorus 1

     B   F#   E
To - day I don't feel like doin' an - ything.

     B   F#   E
I just wanna lay in my bed.

       B   F#
Don't feel like pickin' up ____ my phone,

     E
So leave a message at the tone

         B   D#7   E   N.C.
'Cause to - day I swear I'm not doin' an - ything. Ah.

Verse 1

       B   F#
I'm gonna kick my feet up then stare at the fan,

     E
Turn the TV on, throw my hand in my pants.

     B   F#   E
Nobody's goin' tell me I can't, ____ no.

       B   F#
I'll be loungin' on the couch just chillin' in my Snuggie,

     E
Click to MTV so they can teach me how to dougie.

       B   F#   E
'Cause in my castle, I'm the frickin' ____ man.

Pre-Chorus 1

      C#m   D#m
Oh, yes, I said it,   I said it.

    E   F#
I said it 'cause I can.

Chorus 2

      B   F#   E
To - day I don't feel like doin' an - ything.

      B   F#   E
I just wanna lay in my bed.

        B   F#
Don't feel like pickin' up ____ my phone,

      E
So leave a message at the tone

        B   D#7   E   N.C.
'Cause to - day I swear I'm not doin' an - ything, noth - in' at all.

Interlude

B   F#   E   B
  (Woo, hoo,   woo, hoo, hoo.) Nothin' at all.

        F#   E
(Woo, hoo,   woo, hoo, hoo.)

Verse 2

        B   F#
Tomorrow I'll wake up, do some P-Ninety-X,

      E
Meet a really nice girl, have some really nice sex.

     B   F#   E
And she's gonna scream out, "This is great!" __

(Oh my God, this is great.)

       B   F#
Yeah, I might mess around and get my college degree.

    E
I bet my old man will be so proud of me.

     B   F#   E
But sorry, Pops, you'll just have to wait.

Pre-Chorus 2   *Repeat Pre-Chorus 1*

Chorus 3

B   F#   E
To - day I don't feel like doin' an - ything.

B   F#   E
I just wanna lay in my bed.

      B   F#
Don't feel like pickin' up ____ my phone,

   E
So leave a message at the tone

        B   D#7   E
'Cause to - day I swear I'm not doin' an - ything.

Bridge

N.C. C#m   F#*
  No, I ain't gonna comb my hair

    G#m
'Cause I ain't goin' anywhere,

C#m   F#*   G#m
No, no, no, no, no, no, no, no, no, oh.

    C#m   F#*
I'll just strut in my birthday suit

    G#m
And let ev'rything hang loose,

C#m   F#*   G#m
Yeah, yeah, yeah, yeah, yeah, yeah, yeah, yeah, yeah, yeah.

Chorus 4

N.C.   B   F#   E
  Oh, to - day I don't feel like doin' an - ything.

B   F#   E
I just wanna lay in my bed.

    B   F#
Don't feel like pickin' up ____ my phone,

  E
So leave a message at the tone

       B   D#7   E   N.C.
'Cause to - day I swear I'm not doin' an - ything, noth - in' at all.

Outro

B   F#   E   B
  (Woo, hoo, woo, hoo, hoo.) Nothin' at all.

      F#   E   N.C.
(Woo, hoo, woo, hoo, hoo.) Nothin' at all.

Locked Out of Heaven

Words and Music by Bruno Mars,
Ari Levine and Philip Lawrence

Melody:

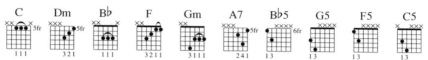

Oh, yeah, _ yeah.   Oh, yeah, _ yeah,

| C | Dm | Bb | F | Gm | A7 | Bb5 | G5 | F5 | C5 |

Intro

C Dm C Bb
Oh, yeah, yeah.

F Gm   C Dm
Oh, yeah, yeah, yeah, yeah.

C Bb
Oh, yeah, yeah.

F Gm   C Dm
Oh, yeah, yeah, yeah, yeah.

Verse 1

        C   Bb
Never had much faith

     F Gm   C Dm
In love or miracles.

        C Bb
Never wan - na put my heart

F   Gm   C Dm
On the line.

         C   Bb
But swimmin' in your world

        F   Gm   C Dm
Is some - thin' spiritual.

        C   Bb
I am born again ev'ry time

       F   Gm
You spend the night.

Pre-Chorus 1

     C   Dm   C B♭
'Cause your sex takes me to paradise.

    F   Gm   F
Yeah, your sex takes me to paradise and it shows.

        A7
Yeah, ___ yeah, yeah.

Chorus 1

                  B♭5   G5
'Cause you make me feel like I've been locked outta heav - en

        F5   C5
For too long, for too long

                B♭5   G5
Yeah, you make me feel like I've been locked outta heav - en

        F5   C5
For too long, for too long,

   C Dm   C B♭
Oh, oh, oh, oh.

Interlude

F Gm   C Dm
Oh, yeah, yeah, yeah, yeah.

C B♭
Oh, yeah, yeah.

F Gm   C Dm
Oh, yeah, yeah, yeah, yeah.

Verse 2

N.C.(Dm)   (C) (B♭)
  You bring me to my   knees,

        (F) (Gm) C Dm
You make me   testify.

         C B♭   F Gm
You can make a   sinner change his ways.

C   Dm   C   B♭
Open up your gates 'cause I can't wait

F Gm   C Dm
To see the light.

         C B♭   F Gm
And right there is where I wan - na stay.

Pre-Chorus 2   *Repeat Pre-Chorus 1*

Chorus 2

Bb5   G5
'Cause you make me feel like I've been locked outta heav - en

F5   C5
For too long, for too long.

Bb5   G5
Yeah, you make me feel like I've been locked outta heav - en

F5   C5   N.C.
For too long, for too long,

Bridge

Bb5
‖: Oh, oo, whoa, oo, whoa, oo, whoa.

G5
Yeah, yeah, yeah.

F5   C5
Can I just stay here, spend the rest of my days here? :‖

Chorus 3

Bb5   G5
'Cause you make me feel like I've been locked outta heav - en

F5   C5
For too long, for too long.

Bb5   G5
Yeah, you make me feel like I've been locked outta heav - en

F5   C5   C Dm
For too long, for too long, oh, oh, oh, oh.

Outro

C Bb F Gm   C Dm
    Oh, yeah, yeah, yeah, yeah.

C Bb
Oh, yeah, yeah.

F Gm   C Dm
Oh, yeah, yeah, yeah, yeah.

Marry You

Words and Music by Bruno Mars,
Ari Levine and Philip Lawrence

It's a beau-ti-ful night. _

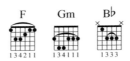

Intro

| F | | | Gm | | |
| Bb | | | F | | |

Chorus 1

       F
It's a beautiful night.

                    Gm
We're looking for something dumb to do.

      Bb   **F**
Hey, ba - by, I think I wanna marry you.

                        Gm
Is it the look in your eyes, or is it this dancing juice?

      Bb   **F**
Who cares, ____ baby, I think I wanna marry you.

Verse 1

         F   **Gm**
Well, I know this little chapel on the boulevard, we can go.

      Bb   **F**
No one will know. Oh, come on, ____ girl.

                                           Gm
Who cares if we're trashed, got a pocket full of cash we can blow.

      Bb   **F**
Shots of Pa - trón and it's on, ____ girl.

Pre-Chorus 1

        F
Don't say, "No, no, no, no, no."

     Gm
Just say, "Yeah, yeah, yeah, yeah, yeah,"

    Bb   **F**
And we'll go, go, go, go, go, if you're read - y like I'm ready.

Cause…

Chorus 2   *Repeat Chorus 1*

Verse 2

F   **Gm**
I'll go get a ring, let the choir bells sing, like, "Ooh."

    Bb   **F**
So, what you wanna do? Let's just run, ____ girl.

                      Gm
If we wake up and you wanna break up, that's cool.

    Bb   **F**
No, I won't blame you, it was fun, ____ girl.

Pre-Chorus 2   *Repeat Pre-Chorus 1*

Chorus 3   *Repeat Chorus 1*

Bridge

    F   **Gm**   **Bb**
Just say, "I do." ____ Tell me right now, baby.

     F
Tell me right now, baby.

         Gm   **Bb**
Baby, just say, "I do." ____ Tell me right now, baby.

     F
Tell me right now, baby, baby.

Oh…

Outro-Chorus   *Repeat Chorus 1*

Moonshine

Words and Music by Bruno Mars,
Ari Levine, Philip Lawrence,
Jeff Bhasker, Andrew Wyatt
and Mark Ronson

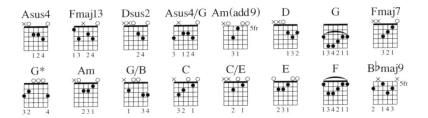

Intro

| Asus4 | | Fmaj13 | | |
| Dsus2 | | Asus4 | Asus4/G | |

Am(add9)

Verse 1   Hello.   You know, you look even better

　　　　　　　　　　　　　　　　　　Fmaj13
Than the way you did the night before.

And the moment you kiss my lips,

　　　　　　　　　　　　　D
You know I start to feel won - derful.

　　　　　　　　　　　Am(add9)　　　　　　**G**
It's something incredible, there's sex in your chemicals, oh.

Verse 2

Am(add9)   Fmaj13
Ooh, let's go. You're the best way I know to escape the extraor - dinary.

This world ain't for you,

                                    D
And I know for damn sure this world ___ ain't for me.

                    Am(add9)   G
Lift off and say goodbye,   just let your fire set me free.

Chorus 1

            Am(add9)   Fmaj13
Oh, moonshine, take us to the stars tonight.

                    D
Take us to that special place,

                    Am(add9)   G
That place we went the last time, the last time.

Verse 3

            Am(add9)
I know,   I was with you last night,

                              Fmaj13
But it feels like it's been so long.

And ev'rybody that's around me knows

                        D
That I'm not myself ___ when you're gone.

                    Am(add9)   G
It's good to see you again,   good to see you again.

Verse 4

            Am(add9)
On top of the world ___ is where I stand

            Fmaj13
When you're back in my life.

                              D
Life's not so bad when you're way up this high.

            Am(add9)   G
Ev'rything is alright,   ev'rything is alright.

Chorus 2

Am(add9)   **Fmaj13**
Oh, moonshine, take us to the stars tonight.

             D
Take us to that special place,

                 Am(add9)   **G**
That place we went the last time, the last time.

      Am(add9)   **Fmaj13**
Oh, moonshine, your loving makes me come alive.

             D
Take us to that special place,

                 Am(add9)   **G**
That place we went the last time, the last time.

Bridge

Fmaj7   **G***   **Am**   **G/B**
Don't look down, don't you never look back.

C   **C/E Fmaj7**
Me, I'm not afraid to die   young and live fast.

                G*   **Am**   **G/B**
Give me good times, give me love, give me laughs.

C   **D**   **E**
  Let's take a ride though the sky

     D   **E**   **F**   **G** **B♭maj9**
Be - fore the night is   gone.

Chorus 3   *Repeat Chorus 2*

Outro

| Am(add9) | | | Fmaj13 | | |
| D | | | Am(add9) | G | *Fade out* |

Natalie

Words and Music by Bruno Mars,
Ari Levine, Philip Lawrence,
Paul Epworth and Benjamin Levin

Melody:

Lord, nev - er done this be - fore, _

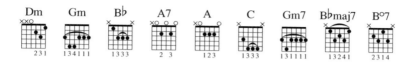

Dm   Gm   B♭   A7   A   C   Gm7   B♭maj7   B°7

Intro   ‖: **Dm** | | | :‖

Verse 1
Dm
    Lord, never done this before,

Never wanna do this again.

Wrong turn on a dusty road.

I did it to myself, I can't pretend.
Gm
    Well, I learned just a little too late.

Good God, I must've been blind,
B♭
    'Cause she got maybe ev'rything,
      A7
Ev - 'rything, ev'rything alright.

Verse 2

Dm
   Like my daddy, I'm a gamblin' man.

Never been afraid to roll the dice.

But when I put my bet on her,

Little Miss Snake Eyes ruined my life.

Gm
   She'd better sleep with one eye open,

Better make sure to lock her doors,

B♭   **A**
   'Cause once I get my hands on her, I'm a ooh!

Chorus 1

Dm   **B♭**   **C**
Natalie. She ran a - way with all my money,

               Gm7
And she did it for fu - u - un.

Dm   **B♭**
Natalie. She's prob'bly out there thinkin'

      C   **Gm7**
It's funny, tellin' ev'ry - o - o - one.

          Dm   **B♭maj7**
Well, ____ I'm diggin' my ditch   for this gold diggin' bitch.

C
   Watch out, she's quick.

Gm7   **Dm**
   Look out for a pretty little thing named Natalie.

      B♭   **C**
If you see her, tell her I'm comin'.

             Gm7
She'd better ru - u - un.

Interlude   ‖: **Dm** | | | :‖

Verse 3

Dm
    The good Lord better bless your soul,

'Cause I've done already cursed your name.

Don't matter which way you go,

Payback's gonna come your way.
Gm
    You'll be begging me, please, please, please,

And I'm gon' look at you and laugh, laugh, laugh
B♭
    While you sit there and cry for me,
        A7
And cry for me, and cry for me all night.

Verse 4

Dm
    I'll spend a lifetime in jail. (Yeah, that's what I'll do.)

I'll be smiling in my cell. (Yeah, thinkin' 'bout you.)
Gm
    Can't nobody save you now, so there ain't no use in tryin'.
B♭   **A**
    Once I get my hands on you, I'm a ooh!

Chorus 2   *Repeat Chorus 1*

Bridge

    B♭maj7
I should've known better (I should've known better)
        Gm7
'Cause when we were together ('Cause when we were together)
    B♭maj7
She never said forever. (She never said forever.)
        B°7   **C**
I'm the fool ____ that paid in her game. ____ Hey!

Chorus 3   *Repeat Chorus 1*

Outro   ‖: **Dm** | | | :‖

            | | ‖

Talking to the Moon

Melody:

I know you're some-where out there,

Words and Music by Bruno Mars,
Ari Levine, Philip Lawrence,
Jeff Bhasker and Albert Winkler

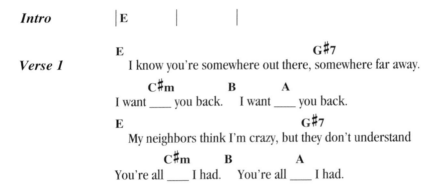

| E | G#7 | C#m | B | A | F#m |
| B/D# | F# | F#m7 | Bsus4 | Emaj9 |

Intro | E | | |

Verse 1

        E   G#7
I know you're somewhere out there, somewhere far away.

   C#m   B   A
I want ____ you back.   I want ____ you back.

E   G#7
My neighbors think I'm crazy, but they don't understand

             C#m   B   A
You're all ____ I had.   You're all ____ I had.

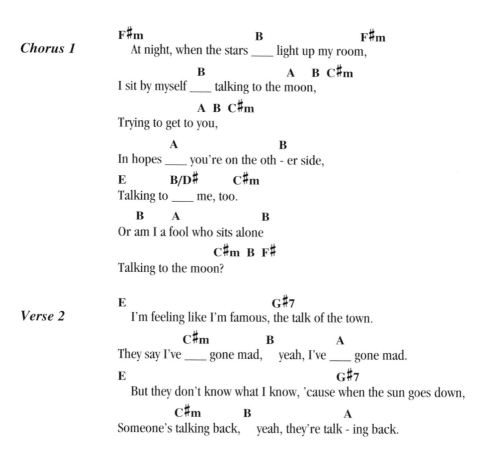

Chorus 1

F#m   B   F#m

  At night, when the stars ____ light up my room,

                B   A   B C#m

I sit by myself ____ talking to the moon,

                A B C#m

Trying to get to you,

           A   B

In hopes ____ you're on the oth - er side,

E   B/D#   C#m

Talking to ____ me, too.

   B   A   B

Or am I a fool who sits alone

                C#m B F#

Talking to the moon?

Verse 2

E   G#7

  I'm feeling like I'm famous, the talk of the town.

           C#m   B   A

They say I've ____ gone mad,   yeah, I've ____ gone mad.

E   G#7

  But they don't know what I know, 'cause when the sun goes down,

           C#m   B   A

Someone's talking back,   yeah, they're talk - ing back.

Chorus 2

F#m   B   F#m
   At night, when the stars ___ light up my room,

         B   A   B C#m
I sit by myself ___ talking to the moon,

         A   B   C#m
Trying to get to you,

        A   B
In hopes ___ you're on the oth - er side,

E   B/D#   C#m
Talking to ___ me, too.

  B   A   B
Or am I a fool who sits alone

            F#m7
Talking to the moon?

Bridge

F#m7   E   F#m7
 (Ah,   ah,   ah.)

Bsus4   B
Do you ever hear me calling?

F#m7   Emaj9   F#m7
 (Ah,   ah,   ah.)
     Oh, oh, oh,   oh, oh, oh.

Chorus 3

      B   N.C.   A   B
'Cause ev'ry night I'm talking to the moon,

C#m   A   B   C#m
  Still trying to get to you,

      A   B
In hopes ___ you're on the oth - er side,

E   B/D#   C#m
Talking to ___ me, too.

  B   A   B
Or am I a fool who sits alone

          C#m B F#
Talking to the moon?

Outro

E   G#7
   I know you're out there somewhere, somewhere far away.

When I Was Your Man

Words and Music by Bruno Mars,
Ari Levine, Philip Lawrence and
Andrew Wyatt

Melody:

Same bed, but it feels just a lit-tle bit big - ger now. _

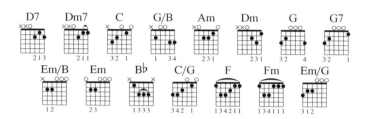

Intro |D7 Dm7 |C |D7 Dm7 |C   G/B |

Verse 1

      Am   C   Dm
Same bed, but it feels just a little bit big - ger now.

      G   G7   C   Em/B
Our song on the radio, but it don't sound ____ the same.

      Am   C   Dm
When our friends talk a - bout you, all it does is just tear ____ me down,

      G   C
'Cause my heart breaks a little when I hear ____ your name.

Pre-Chorus 1

Em/B		Am	Em

It all sounds like, "Ooh, hoo."

	Bb		C/G

Mm, ____ too young, too dumb to realize

Chorus 1

	G N.C.		F	G		C

That I ____ should've bought you flow - ers   and held your hand.

		F	G		C

Should've gave you all my hours ____   when I had the chance.

	F		G		Am

Take you to ev'ry par - ty 'cause all you want - ed to do was dance.

D7		F

Now ____ my baby's danc - ing,

	Fm		C F C Em/B

But she's dancing with another man.

Verse 2

Am		C		Dm

My pride, my ego, my needs and my self - ish ways

G		G7		C	Em/B

Caused a good strong woman like you to walk out ____ my life.

	Am	C		Dm

Now I'm never, nev - er get to clean up the mess ____ I've made,

	G		C

Oh,   and it haunts me ev'ry time I close my eyes.

Pre-Chorus 2   *Repeat Pre-Chorus 1*

Chorus 2

        G N.C.   F   G   C
That I ____ should've bought you flow - ers   and held your hand.

                                   F   G   C
Should've gave you all my hours ____   when I had the chance.

                     F   G   Am
Take you to ev'ry par - ty 'cause all you want - ed to do was dance.

        D7   F
Now ____ my baby's danc - ing,

        Fm   C
But she's dancing with another man.

Bridge

               F
Although it hurts,

        G   C   G/B Am Em/G
I'll be the first to say that I was wrong.

        D7
Oh, I know I'm prob'ly much too late

            Dm7
To try and a - pologize for my mistakes,

           G
But I just want ____ you to know,

Outro-Chorus

N.C.   F   G   C
I hope he buys you flowers,   I hope he holds your hand,

            F   G   C
Give you all his hours   when he has ____ the chance.

                   F   G
Take you to ev'ry par - ty, 'cause I re - member

                Am
How much you love to dance.

D7   F   Fm   C
Do all the things I ____ should've done   when I was your man.

D7   F   Fm   C
Do all the things I ____ should've done   when I was your man.

Treasure

Words and Music by Bruno Mars,
Ari Levine, Philip Lawrence,
Fredrick Brown and Thibaut Berland

Melody:

Gim-me your, gim-me your, gim-me your at-ten-tion, ba - by.

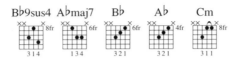

Bb9sus4 Abmaj7 Bb Ab Cm

Intro

Bb9sus4 | |

Verse 1

Abmaj7   Bb   Ab
Gimme your, gimme your, gimme your atten - tion, baby.

Abmaj7 Bb   Cm
    I gotta tell you a little somethin' about your - self.

Bb   Abmaj7   Bb   Ab
  You're wonderful, flawless, ooh, you're a sex - y lady,

Abmaj7 Bb   Cm
  But you walk around here like you wanna be someone ____ else.

Pre-Chorus 1

Bb Abmaj7 Bb Ab
Oh, whoa, _____ I know that you don't know it,

Abmaj7 Bb   Cm
But you're fine, so fine.   (Fine, so fine.)

Bb Abmaj7 Bb Ab
Oh, whoa, _____ oh, girl, I'm gonna show you

Abmaj7   Bb9sus4
When you're mine, all mine. (Mine, all mine.)

Chorus 1

A♭maj7 B♭ A♭   A♭maj7 B♭
Treasure.   That is what you are.

    Cm   B♭ A♭maj7
Hon - ey, you're my gold - en star,

B♭   A♭   A♭maj7 B♭
You know you can make my wish come true,

  Cm   B♭   A♭maj7
If you let me treas - ure you,

B♭ A♭   B♭9sus4
  If you let me treasure, oh, oh, oh.

Verse 2

A♭maj7   B♭   A♭
Pretty girl, pretty girl, pretty girl, you should be smilin'.

A♭maj7 B♭   Cm
   A girl like you should never look so ___ blue.

B♭   A♭maj7 B♭ A♭
You're ev - 'rything ___ I see in my dreams.

A♭maj7 B♭   Cm
   I wouldn't say that to you if it wasn't ___ true.

Pre-Chorus 2   *Repeat Pre-Chorus 1*

Chorus 2   *Repeat Chorus 1*

Bridge

A♭maj7   B♭ A♭   A♭maj7
  You are my treas - ure,   you are my treasure,

B♭   Cm   B♭
  You are my treasure, yeah, you, you, you, you are.

A♭maj7   B♭ A♭   A♭maj7
  You are my treas - ure,   you are my treasure,

B♭9sus4
  You are my treasure, yeah, you, you, you, you are.

Chorus 3   *Repeat Chorus 1*

Outro

‖: A♭maj7   B♭ A♭ | A♭maj7 |
| B♭   Cm | B♭ :‖ *Repeat and fade*

Young Girls

Words and Music by Bruno Mars,
Ari Levine, Philip Lawrence,
Jeff Bhasker and Emile Haynie

I spend all ___ my ___ mon - ey

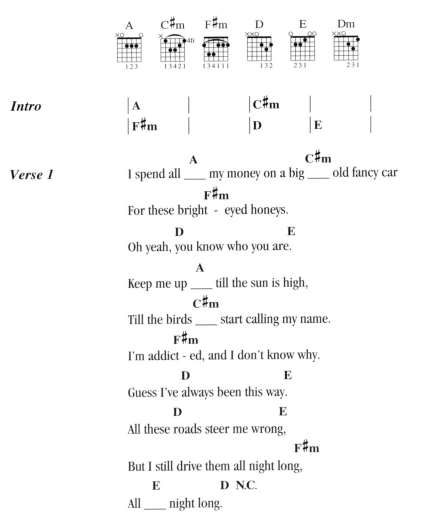

Intro

| A | | | C#m | | |
| F#m | | | D | | E | |

Verse 1

      A   **C#m**
I spend all ___ my money on a big ___ old fancy car

     F#m
For these bright - eyed honeys.

     D   **E**
Oh yeah, you know who you are.

     A
Keep me up ___ till the sun is high,

     C#m
Till the birds ___ start calling my name.

   F#m
I'm addict - ed, and I don't know why.

     D   **E**
Guess I've always been this way.

     D   **E**
All these roads steer me wrong,

                        F#m
But I still drive them all night long,

   E   **D N.C.**
All ___ night long.

Chorus 1

A   C#m

All you young, ___ wild girls, you make a mess ___ of me.

     F#m

Yeah, you young, ___ wild girls,

        D   E

You'll be the death ___ of me, the death ___ of me.

      A   C#m

All you young, ___ wild girls, no matter what ___ you do,

     F#m   D

Yeah, you young, ___ wild girls, I always come back ___ to you,

    C#m   E   A

Come back ___ to you.

Verse 2

     A   C#m

I get lost ___ under these lights, I get lost ___ in the words I say,

    F#m   D   E

Start believ - ing my own lies like ev'ry - thing will be okay.

    A

Oh, I ___ still dream of a simple life;

  C#m

Boy ___ meets girl, makes her his wife.

  F#m

But love don't exist when you live like this,

       D   E

That much I know, ___ yes, I know.

     D   E

All these roads steer me wrong,

           F#m

But I still drive them all night long,

E   D N.C.(Dm)

All night long.

Chorus 2

               A   **C♯m**
All you young, ___ wild girls, you make a mess ___ of me.

                     F♯m
Yeah, you young, ___ wild girls,

                    D   **E**
You'll be the death ___ of me, the death ___ of me.

               A   **C♯m**
All you young, ___ wild girls, no matter what ___ you do,

                     F♯m
Yeah, you young, ___ wild girls,

                    D   **C♯m**   **E**
I always come back ___ to you, come back ___ to you.

Bridge

 A   **C♯m**
  You, you, ooh, ___ ooh, woo.

  F♯m   **D**
You, ___ you, you, ooh, ___ ooh, woo.

E   **A**   **C♯m**
  Yeah, you, ___ you, you, ooh, ___ ooh, woo.

  F♯m   **D**
You, ___ you, you, ___ ooh, woo.

Chorus 3

C♯m **E**   **A**   **C♯m**
      All you young, ___ wild girls, you make a mess ___ of me.

                 F♯m
Yeah, you young, ___ wild girls,

                   D   **E**
You'll be the death ___ of me, the death ___ of me.

               A   **C♯m**
All you young, ___ wild girls, no matter what ___ you do,

                 F♯m   **D**
Yeah, you young, ___ wild girls, I always come back ___ to you,

        C♯m   **E**   **A**
Come back ___ to you.

Guitar Chord Songbooks

Each book includes complete lyrics, chord symbols, and guitar chord diagrams.

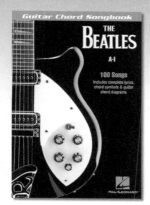

Acoustic Hits
More than 60 songs: Against the Wind • Name • One • Southern Cross • Take Me Home, Country Roads • Teardrops on My Guitar • Who'll Stop the Rain • Ziggy Stardust • and more.
00701787 ....$14.99

Acoustic Rock
80 acoustic favorites: Blackbird • Blowin' in the Wind • Layla • Maggie May • Me and Julio down by the Schoolyard • Pink Houses • and more.
00699540..............................$17.95

Adele
Over 30 songs: Chasing Pavements • I Can't Make You Love Me • Make You Feel My Love • Rolling in the Deep • Rumour Has It • Someone like You • and more.
00102761..............................$14.99

Alabama
50 of Alabama's best: Born Country • Dixieland Delight • Feels So Right • Mountain Music • Song of the South • Why Lady Why • and more.
00699914 ....$14.95

The Beach Boys
59 favorites: California Girls • Don't Worry Baby • Fun, Fun, Fun • Good Vibrations • Help Me Rhonda • Wouldn't It Be Nice • dozens more!
00699566..............................$14.95

The Beatles (A-I)
An awesome reference of Beatles hits: All You Need Is Love • The Ballad of John and Yoko • Get Back • Good Day Sunshine • A Hard Day's Night • Hey Jude • I Saw Her Standing There • and more!
00699558..............................$17.99

The Beatles (J-Y)
100 more Beatles hits: Lady Madonna • Let It Be • Ob-La-Di, Ob-La-Da • Paperback Writer • Revolution • Twist and Shout • When I'm Sixty-Four • and more.
00699562..............................$17.99

Bluegrass
Over 40 classics: Blue Moon of Kentucky • Foggy Mountain Top • High on a Mountain Top • Keep on the Sunny Side • Wabash Cannonball • The Wreck of the Old '97 • and more.
00702585..............................$14.99

Blues
80 blues tunes: Big Boss Man • Cross Road Blues (Crossroads) • Damn Right, I've Got the Blues • Pride and Joy • Route 66 • Sweet Home Chicago • and more.
00699733 ....$12.95

Broadway
80 stage hits: All I Ask of You • Bali Ha'i • Edelweiss • Hello, Dolly! • Memory • Ol' Man River • People • Seasons of Love • Sunrise, Sunset • and more.
00699920 ....$14.99

Johnny Cash
58 Cash classics: A Boy Named Sue • Cry, Cry, Cry • Daddy Sang Bass • Folsom Prison Blues • I Walk the Line • RIng of Fire • Solitary Man • and more.
00699648..............................$17.99

Steven Curtis Chapman
65 from this CCM superstar: Be Still and Know • Cinderella • For the Sake of the Call • Live Out Loud • Speechless • With Hope • and more.
00700702 ....$17.99

Children's Songs
70 songs for kids: Alphabet Song • Bingo • The Candy Man • Eensy Weensy Spider • Puff the Magic Dragon • Twinkle, Twinkle Little Star • and more!
00699539..............................$16.99

Christmas Carols
80 Christmas carols: Angels We Have Heard on High • The Holly and the Ivy • I Saw Three Ships • Joy to the World • O Holy Night • and more.
00699536..............................$12.99

Christmas Songs – 2nd Ed.
80 songs: All I Want for Christmas Is My Two Front Teeth • Baby, It's Cold Outside • Jingle Bell Rock • Mistletoe and Holly • Sleigh Ride • and more.
00119911..............................$14.99

Eric Clapton
75 of Slowhand's finest: I Shot the Sheriff • Knockin' on Heaven's Door • Layla • Strange Brew • Tears in Heaven • Wonderful Tonight • and more!
00699567..............................$15.99

Classic Rock
80 rock essentials: Beast of Burden • Cat Scratch Fever • Hot Blooded • Money • Rhiannon • Sweet Emotion • Walk on the Wild Side • more
00699598 ....$15.99

Coffeehouse Hits
57 singer-songwriter hits: Don't Know Why • Hallelujah • Meet Virginia • Steal My Kisses • Torn • Wonderwall • You Learn • and more.
00703318 ....$14.99

Country
80 country standards: Boot Scootin' Boogie • Crazy • Hey, Good Lookin' • Sixteen Tons • Through the Years • Your Cheatin' Heart • more.
00699534..............................$14.95

Country Favorites
Over 60 songs: Achy Breaky Heart (Don't Tell My Heart) • Brand New Man • Gone Country • The Long Black Veil • Make the World Go Away • and more.
00700609 ....$14.99

Country Standards
60 songs: By the Time I Get to Phoenix • El Paso • The Gambler • I Fall to Pieces • Jolene • King of the Road • Put Your Hand in the Hand • A Rainy Night in Georgia • more.
00700608 ....$12.95

Cowboy Songs
Over 60 tunes: Back in the Saddle Again • Happy Trails • Home on the Range • Streets of Laredo • The Yellow Rose of Texas • and more.
00699636 ....$12.95

Creedence Clearwater Revival
34 CCR classics: Bad Moon Rising • Born on the Bayou • Down on the Corner • Fortunate Son • Up Around the Bend • and more!
00701786 ....$12.99

Crosby, Stills & Nash
37 hits: Chicago • Dark Star • Deja Vu • Marrakesh Express • Our House • Southern Cross • Suite: Judy Blue Eyes • Teach Your Children • and more.
00701609................................$12.99

John Denver
50 favorites: Annie's Song • Leaving on a Jet Plane • Rocky Mountain High • Take Me Home, Country Roads • Thank God I'm a Country Boy • and more.
02501697 ....$14.99

Neil Diamond
50 songs: America • Cherry, Cherry • Cracklin' Rosie • Forever in Blue Jeans • I Am...I Said • Love on the Rocks • Song Sung Blue • Sweet Caroline • and dozens more!
00700606 ....$14.99

Disney
56 super Disney songs: Be Our Guest • Friend like Me • Hakuna Matata • It's a Small World • Under the Sea • A Whole New World • Zip-A-Dee-Doo-Dah • and more!
00701071 ....$14.99

The Best of Bob Dylan
70 Dylan classics: Blowin' in the Wind • Forever Young • Hurricane • It Ain't Me Babe • Just like a Woman • Lay Lady Lay • Like a Rolling Stone • and more.
14037617 ....$17.99

Folk Pop Rock
80 songs: American Pie • Dust in the Wind • Me and Bobby McGee • Somebody to Love • Time in a Bottle • and more.
00699651 ....$14.95

Folksongs
80 folk favorites: Aura Lee • Camptown Races • Danny Boy • Man of Constant Sorrow • Nobody Knows the Trouble I've Seen • and more.
00699541 ....$12.95

40 Easy Strumming Songs
Features 40 songs: Cat's in the Cradle • Daughter • Hey, Soul Sister • Homeward Bound • Take It Easy • Wild Horses • and more.
00115972 ....$14.99

Four Chord Songs
40 hit songs: Blowin' in the Wind • I Saw Her Standing There • Should I Stay or Should I Go • Stand by Me • Turn the Page • Wonderful Tonight • and more.
00701611 ....$12.99

Glee
50+ hits: Bad Romance • Beautiful • Dancing with Myself • Don't Stop Believin' • Imagine • Rehab • Teenage Dream • True Colors • and dozens more.
00702501 ....$14.99

Gospel Hymns
80 hymns: Amazing Grace • Give Me That Old Time Religion • I Love to Tell the Story • Shall We Gather at the River? • Wondrous Love • and more.
00700463 ....$14.99

Grand Ole Opry®
80 great songs: Abilene • Act Naturally • Country Boy • Crazy • Friends in Low Places • He Stopped Loving Her Today • Wings of a Dove • dozens more!
00699885 ....$16.95

Guitar Chord Songbook White Pages
400 songs in over 1,000 pages! Includes: California Girls • Footloose • Hey Jude • King of the Road • Man in the Mirror • and many more.
00702609................................$29.99

Hillsong United
65 top worship songs: Break Free • Everyday • From the Inside Out • God Is Great • Look to You • Now That You're Near • Salvation Is Here • To the Ends of the Earth • and more.
00700222 ....$12.95

Irish Songs
45 Irish favorites: Danny Boy • Girl I Left Behind Me • Harrigan • I'll Tell Me Ma • The Irish Rover • My Wild Irish Rose • When Irish Eyes Are Smiling • and more!
00701044 ....$14.99

Billy Joel
60 Billy Joel favorites: • It's Still Rock and Roll to Me • The Longest Time • Piano Man • She's Always a Woman • Uptown Girl • We Didn't Start the Fire • You May Be Right • and more.
00699632 ....$15.99

Elton John
60 songs: Bennie and the Jets • Candle in the Wind • Crocodile Rock • Goodbye Yellow Brick Road • Pinball Wizard • Sad Songs (Say So Much) • Tiny Dancer • Your Song • and more.
00699732 ....$15.99

Latin Songs
60 favorites: Bésame Mucho (Kiss Me Much) • The Girl from Ipanema (Garôta De Ipanema) • The Look of Love • So Nice (Summer Samba) • and more.
00700973 ....$14.99

Love Songs
65 romantic ditties: Baby, I'm-A Want You • Fields of Gold • Here, There and Everywhere • Let's Stay Together • Never My Love • The Way We Were • more!
00701043................................$14.99

Bob Marley
36 songs: Buffalo Soldier • Get up Stand Up • I Shot the Sheriff • Is This Love • No Woman No Cry • One Love • Redemption Song • and more.
00701704................................$12.99

Paul McCartney
60 from Sir Paul: Band on the Run • Jet • Let 'Em In • Maybe I'm Amazed • No More Lonely Nights • Say Say Say • Take It Away • With a Little Luck • more!
00385035 ....$16.95

Steve Miller
33 hits: Dance Dance Dance • Jet Airliner • The Joker • Jungle Love • Rock'n Me • Serenade from the Stars • Swingtown • Take the Money and Run • and more.
00701146................................$12.99

Modern Worship
80 modern worship favorites: All Because of Jesus • Amazed • Everlasting God • Happy Day • I Am Free • Jesus Messiah • and more.
00701801 ....$16.99

Motown
60 Motown masterpieces: ABC • Baby I Need Your Lovin' • I'll Be There • Stop! In the Name of Love • You Can't Hurry Love • more.
00699734 ....$16.95

The 1950s
80 early rock favorites: High Hopes • Mister Sandman • Only You (And You Alone) • Put Your Head on My Shoulder • Tammy • That's Amoré • and more.
00699922 ....$14.99

The 1980s
80 hits: Centerfold • Come on Eileen • Don't Worry, Be Happy • Got My Mind Set on You • Sailing • Should I Stay or Should I Go • Sweet Dreams (Are Made of This) • more.
00700551 ....$16.99

Nirvana
40 songs: About a Girl • Come as You Are • Heart Shaped Box • The Man Who Sold the World • Smells like Teen Spirit • You Know You're Right • and more.
00699762 ....$16.99

Roy Orbison
38 songs: Blue Bayou • Oh, Pretty Woman • Only the Lonely (Know the Way I Feel) • Working for the Man • You Got It • and more.
00699752 ....$12.95

Peter, Paul & Mary
43 favorites: If I Had a Hammer (The Hammer Song) • Leaving on a Jet Plane • Puff the Magic Dragon • This Land Is Your Land • and more.
00103013................................$12.99

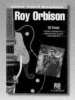

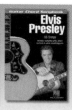

Tom Petty
American Girl • Breakdown • Don't Do Me like That • Free Fallin' • Here Comes My Girl • Into the Great Wide Open • Mary Jane's Last Dance • Refugee • Runnin' Down a Dream • The Waiting • more.
00699883 ....$15.99

Pop/Rock
80 chart hits: Against All Odds • Come Sail Away • Every Breath You Take • Hurts So Good • Kokomo • More Than Words • Smooth • Summer of '69 • more.
00699538 ....$14.95

Praise and Worship
80 favorites: Agnus Dei • He Is Exalted • I Could Sing of Your Love Forever • Lord, I Lift Your Name on High • More Precious Than Silver • Open the Eyes of My Heart • Shine, Jesus, Shine • and more.
00699634 ....$14.99

Elvis Presley
60 hits: All Shook Up • Blue Suede Shoes • Can't Help Falling in Love • Heartbreak Hotel • Hound Dog • Jailhouse Rock • Suspicious Minds • Viva Las Vegas • more.
00699633 ....$14.95

Queen
40 hits: Bohemian Rhapsody • Crazy Little Thing Called Love • Fat Bottomed Girls • Killer Queen • Tie Your Mother Down • Under Pressure • You're My Best Friend • and more.
00702395 ....$12.99

Red Hot Chili Peppers
50 hits: Californication • Give It Away • Higher Ground • Love Rollercoaster • Scar Tissue • Suck My Kiss • Under the Bridge • and more.
00699710 ....$16.95

Rock Ballads
54 songs: Amanda • Boston • Brick • Landslide • Love Hurts • Mama, I'm Coming Home • She Will Be Loved • Waiting for a Girl like You • and more.
00701034 ....$14.99

Rock 'n' Roll
80 rock 'n' roll classics: At the Hop • Great Balls of Fire • It's My Party • La Bamba • My Boyfriend's Back • Peggy Sue • Stand by Me • more.
00699535 ....$14.95

Bob Seger
41 favorites: Against the Wind • Hollywood Nights • Katmandu • Like a Rock • Night Moves • Old Time Rock & Roll • You'll Accomp'ny Me • and more!
00701147 ....$12.99

Carly Simon
Nearly 40 classic hits, including: Anticipation • Haven't Got Time for the Pain • Jesse • Let the River Run • Nobody Does It Better • You're So Vain • and more.
00121011 ....$14.99

Sting
50 favorites from Sting and the Police: Don't Stand So Close to Me • Every Breath You Take • Fields of Gold • King of Pain • Message in a Bottle • Roxanne • more.
00699921 ....$14.99

Taylor Swift
27 tunes: Fifteen • Hey Stephen • Love Story • Our Song • Picture to Burn • Tim McGraw • Today Was a Fairytale • White Horse • You Belong with Me • and more.
00701799 ....$15.99

Three Chord Songs
65 includes: All Right Now • La Bamba • Lay Down Sally • Mony, Mony • Rock Around the Clock • Rock This Town • Werewolves of London • You Are My Sunshine • and more.
00699720 ....$12.95

Today's Hits
40 of today's top hits, including: Blurred Lines • Call Me Maybe • Cruise • Drive By • Ho Hey • Little Talks • Mirrors • Radioactive • Stay • We Are Young • When I Was Your Man • and more.
00120983 ....$14.99

Top 100 Hymns
100 songs: 'Tis So Sweet to Trust in Jesus • A Mighty Fortress Is Our God • Christ the Lord Is Risen Today • Higher Ground • In the Sweet by and By • Rock of Ages, Cleft for Me • and many more!
75718017 ....$14.99

Two-Chord Songs
Nearly 60 songs: ABC • Brick House • Eleanor Rigby • Fever • Paperback Writer • Ramblin' Man Tulsa Time • When Love Comes to Town • and more.
00119236 ....$14.99

Wedding Songs
50 songs that every gigging musician should know, including: Endless Love • Have I Told You Lately • Longer • Through the Years • and more.
00701005 ....$14.99

Guitar Chord Songbook White Pages
400 songs into one conveniently-sized book: All Along the Watchtower • Back to December • Daydream • Hey Jude • King of the Road • Shout • Uptown Girl • Wild Thing • and many more.
00702609 ....$29.99

Hank Williams
68 classics: Cold, Cold Heart • Hey, Good Lookin' • Honky Tonk Blues • I'm a Long Gone Daddy • Jambalaya (On the Bayou) • Your Cheatin' Heart • and more.
00700607 ....$14.99

Neil Young
35 songs: After the Gold Rush • Cinnamon Girl • Down by the River • Harvest • Heart of Gold • Like a Hurricane • Long May You Run • Ohio • Old Man • Southern Man • and more.
00700464 ....$14.99

Complete contents listings available online at www.halleonard.com